BRIEF LIVES

by

JOHN AUBREY

A Play in Two Acts
for One Player

adapted by

PATRICK GARLAND

FABER AND FABER
24 Russell Square
London

First published in 1967
by Faber and Faber Limited
24 Russell Square London WC1
Reprinted 1969
Printed in Great Britain by
Latimer Trend & Co Ltd Whitstable

SBN (Paper edition) 571 08314 5
SBN (Cloth edition) 571 08313 7

For
ROY DOTRICE

Acknowledgements

In preparing this adaptation of *Brief Lives* for the stage, I was greatly helped by *John Aubrey's Brief Lives* by Oliver Lawson Dick (Secker & Warburg and Peregrine Books), and *John Aubrey and his Friends* by Anthony Powell (Heinemann).

P.G.

Brief Lives was produced first at the Hampstead Theatre Club on January 16th, 1967. It was directed by Patrick Garland, and designed by Julia Trevelyan Oman. John Aubrey was played by Roy Dotrice.

In 1964, a shorter adaptation of part of the writings of John Aubrey, called The Antiquary, appeared on BBC television in the series, Famous Gossips, produced by Patrick Garland with Roy Dotrice in the part of John Aubrey.

An Introduction to John Aubrey

John Aubrey's *Lives* are among the most brilliant of Seventeenth Century memoirs, but the author himself is not widely known. He was born in 1626 in the County of Wiltshire, and he experienced the changing fortunes of the Civil War while an undergraduate at Oxford. At the Restoration of Charles II, John Aubrey was still a young man, and it was not until 1697 that he died, during the reign of William III, aged 71. Like the story he tells himself about "the tragical end of the old church raven", John Aubrey lived through many changes of government and religion. In his youth he inherited a prosperous estate, but he lacked the ability to secure it, and lost everything by the age of forty-five. Most of his life was spent generously collecting scholarly information and scandalous gossip for other people, and he produced a number of literary and antiquarian works, ranging from a *History of Wiltshire* to *An Idea of Education*, but only his book *Miscellanies* was published in his lifetime. His masterpiece remains, unquestionably, his book of *Lives*, which he managed to complete during a lifetime spent in other people's houses, or lodgings, relying on the generosity of good friends and relatives. He says, of himself, that gratitude was his chief virtue, and it seems improbable he was ever an unwelcome guest. The *Lives* were not published until after his death, and it is only in this century that John Aubrey has begun to be recognised as England's first serious biographer, and that he can now take his rightful place alongside Pepys and Evelyn as the greatest chroniclers of their, or indeed any, age.

PATRICK GARLAND

A NOTE on the staging of 'BRIEF LIVES'

When Roy Dotrice and I first decided to work towards a stage-version of John Aubrey's writings, we were both determined to recreate as far as possible the authentic atmosphere of Seventeenth Century daily life, and in collaboration with the designer, Julia Trevelyan Oman, succeeded, I believe, in capturing the essence of what I called "Jacobean kitchen-sink". This was largely helped by the generous loan from friends of genuine seventeenth-century, and earlier, furniture and books. In fact, among the hundreds of old volumes used to litter the stage, there were several dozen which were already antique when Aubrey was born.

Brief Lives attempts to represent a day in the life of John Aubrey when he stayed in lodgings in London in his final years. At the beginning of the play he wakes from a large four-poster bed, and he is sitting before the fire in his nightgown at the end of it. In between, he eats, drinks, reads, writes, washes, chatters, urinates, dozes, all without any self-conscious awareness of the spectators. It is as if one is simply paying a visit to the house of an old man, who lives alone and in some discomfort, and who makes up for the absence of friends by bringing to life reminiscences of people, some famous, some obscure, remembering them and telling stories about them. As he says himself, the greatest pleasure left to an old man is to "renew acquaintance with his old and deceased friends". At the conclusion of Act One, he dozes off in the middle of relating an anecdote about Sir Walter Raleigh—he sleeps in his armchair while the audience leaves during the interval—then, at the beginning of Act Two wakes up, and continues the story. It is essential that the curtain remains up, and that throughout the performance John Aubrey never leaves the stage.

Of course, a naturalistic Jacobean set would mean nothing without Aubrey's text, and the actor's performance; but equally, both text and performance would be reduced without such atmosphere, and with a less-elaborate setting. It was bound to be an expensive and complicated undertaking, but because the set contributed so much to the play, it is worth spending a little time to describe it. The action takes place one winter's day in 1696, at Mistress Byerley's lodgings, Dirty Lane, Bloomsbury. Throughout the day, John Aubrey, aged seventy, is plagued not only by distractions outside his window (revellers, town-criers, street singers) but also by a crying child in the next chamber, a hammering schoolmaster above, and a lute player in the room below. As the first morning light filters through the heavy curtains of John Aubrey's chamber—which serves him as bedroom, library, kitchen and study—it slowly reveals a dusty, untidy, and overcrowded room, more like a museum than a private lodging. For within these walls is the collection of a dedicated antiquary, carefully acquired throughout a lifetime of searching after antiquities and curiosities.

The walls are hung with ancient tapestries, formerly very fine, now worn and faded. On these are paintings of Elizabethan times (an elegant poetic-looking young man, an austere court beauty fashionably dressed), pikes and halberds, muskets, breast-plates, a sundial, coats-of-arms. On the side farthest away from the windows, which overlook the street, Aubrey keeps his kitchen. He collects food in the same way he collects antiquities—there is far more than he needs, and a lot has been left over from former meals. Carcasses of chickens and the remains of fish litter the long table set against the wall, also jugs, and plates of spices, herbs, grain, and seeds. A wooden bowl of unrefined brown sugar (for his claret), another of tobacco, a dish of eggs, dried apricots and shrivelled grapes in a pewter plate, a dozen mackerel on another, an earthenware jug of milk, and some round slices of rye bread. Also books, candlesticks, pages of manuscript, mixed up with the food, smoke-blackened saucepans. Underneath this table Aubrey keeps his fruit and vegetables—large flat baskets of cabbages, potatoes, apples, peaches, pears, and a half-sliced pumpkin, all past their first freshness. Above the table, a long shelf, from which hang three or four chickens, a woodcock, a pair of rabbits, and bundles of herbs, bay leaves, etc. Pewter jugs, mugs, candlesticks and plates stand on the shelf itself.

By the kitchen table is Aubrey's favourite evening chair—

collected from an old Parish church on his former estate in Wiltshire—with a towering back, and wooden canopy. Aubrey is dwarfed when he sits in it. On top of the canopy, a small pile of forgotten books, and an ornate jug and goblet, covered in cobwebs.

Behind the chair is Aubrey's bedchamber, consisting of a large, jumbled four-poster bed with curtains. John Aubrey lies asleep behind these curtains when the play starts. Once the curtains are opened the bed is seen to be much slept in but never aired or made, the bed linen seldom changed. Books, slippers and a warming pan, as well as a pewter chamber-pot lie under the bed, also more books on top of it. Next to this, on a bedside table, the bust of Dame Venetia Stanley, in bronze, covered with dark net.

Below the bed, and almost in the centre of the room, the fireplace, with Aubrey's favourite armchair drawn up to it, and a stool to the right. A poker already set in the fire, chestnuts on the hob, and a small fireside bench on the left of the grate, with Aubrey's tobacco bowl, clay pipes, spills and knife. Between his armchair and the stool, a substantial table, with manuscripts and books as well as candlesticks on it, silver snuffers, and the remains of the previous day's supper. A bronze helmet and a world-globe underneath the table.

At the back of the room, in the centre, is an extensive alcove, dimly lit, in which can be seen more tapestries hanging, and suits of armour and weapons. In front of this, an ancient chest where the antiquary keeps his most precious curiosities, concealed by a cloth, and heavy books on top of it. On the other side of the alcove, is John Aubrey's gallery library, reaching from floor to ceiling, with steps leading up to it, books also stacked on every side, including the stairs. There is a window in the gallery, and another larger window below this, which faces the street, both curtained when the play begins. Also on the stairs a stuffed bear-cub. Aubrey works at a table by this lower window, on which are spread out the manuscripts pertaining to his book of *Lives*, carefully divided into selected piles, but mixed up together with Roman coins, shells, and an astrological globe. A small passage between the long table and the window gives just enough room for Aubrey to reach the desk at which he has been working on his *Idea of Education*. This corner of the room is hardly ever used, and is the dust-covered, cobwebbed receptacle of all his unwanted junk, and bowls of dead flowers.

When the play begins, John Aubrey is asleep in his four-poster bed. His clothes are scattered over the chairs near the fireplace. Deeply rooted in the past, Aubrey even dresses in the fashions of a vanished age. In place of formal Jacobean elegance, a tattered gown with a fur-lined robe, much deteriorated, serves him for everyday dress, and this he pulls straight over his night-shirt. The hem is worn and threadbare where it touches the floor, and the buttoned front is stained with the spilt food and candle wax of years. He wears spectacles, grubby black mittens, and potters around his curiosities with the help of an ebony stick. He is a very fragile old man, short-sighted, unsteady, almost bald with straggly beard and hair, as brittle and as threadbare as a cabbage stalk; in appearance, he looks several decades more ancient than his seventy-one years, but is perky and full of activity.

PATRICK GARLAND

ACT ONE

A winter morning, in the grey hour before dawn. In the distance, a street singer. (His song "Reynardine" is an ancient ballad about a mysterious lover, half-man, half-fox. Experts set its date in Queen Elizabeth's time.)

SINGER: One evening as I rambled
Among the leaves so fine
I overheard a young woman
Conversing with Reynardine.

Her hair was black, her eyes were blue,
Her mouth as red as wine,
And he smiled to look upon her,
Did this sly, bold Reynardine.

(*Early morning light filters through during the second verse of the song. The street singer passes beneath the windows of Aubrey's house, and moves farther away. As his voice fades in the distance, a dog barks. Suddenly, from upstairs, the silence of the dawn is shattered by loud hammering which continues intermittently for several minutes. A group of drunk revellers stagger below the window singing uncouthly "Ye Mariners All" (to be found in "The Penguin Book of English Folk Songs").*

REVELLERS: Ye mariners all, as you pass by,
Call in and drink if you are dry.
Come spend, my lads, your money brisk,
And pop your nose in a jug of this.

(AUBREY *wakes, angrily pulls aside the bed-curtains and peeps out. Barefooted, wrapping shawl round him, he goes to the window and grumbles.*)

AUBREY: Revels . . . ! Revels! Alas, O God's will! Meet at a poor blind sordid alehouse, drink up a barrel of drink, and lie there drunk two or three hours together!

(AUBREY *pulls back curtain, and opening the casement, shouts down to the revellers.*)

Fall together by the ears!

(REVELLER *calls up to the window—"Pop your nose in a good jug of this!"—Drunken laughter.*)

It was not so in Queen Elizabeth's time. Then youth had respect to old age. All this is now lost, and pride, whoreing, wantonesses and drunkennesses!

(*Coaches outside starting and moving off.*)

Alas, O God's will! Nowadays everyone must have coaches, forsooth! It was not so in Queen Elizabeth's time. In those days gentlemen kept good horses, and men at arms, that could ride them. This made the gentry robust and hardy and fit for service. Nowadays, forsooth, we are come to our coaches, forsooth!

(AUBREY *goes over to fire, takes up spectacles from stool and puts them on, takes bellows from fire-dog and bellows up the fire which soon begins to blaze cheerfully.*)

In Queen Elizabeth's time, 'twas as much disgrace for a cavalier to be seen in the streets of London riding in a coach, as 'twould be nowadays to be seen in a petticoat. Nowadays young men know not how to ride, nor to handle their weapons. So God help the king, now we are all come to our coaches . . . forsooth!

(*In the next chamber a baby wakes and cries lustily.*)

God bless me. . . .

(AUBREY *hangs up fire-bellows, takes up his stick which has been lying on the table, and goes over to bang on the wall near the kitchen-shelf. As soon as he starts banging on the wall, the man upstairs starts hammering again.* AUBREY *shakes his head, and going up to the four-poster starts dressing. He puts on his tattered green gown, then wearily collapses on to the bed to start doing up the dozens of buttons. All this time, the hammering and the crying child continue intermittently.*)

One would think there was an evil genius did haunt me. A writing schoolmaster takes the chamber above me: comes in at twelve or one and wakes me out of my sleep, rises very early and falls a-hammering for a quarter of an hour or more —the week after comes a man and his wife, and a child breeding teeth, that cries day and night.

(*In an attempt to avoid the noise, still buttoning his gown,* AUBREY *moves over to the centre of the room and sits on the end of a large chest by the staircase, which contains all his greatest treasures. During this time, the noise ceases by degrees.*)

'Twas a great disadvantage to me in my childhood to be pent up in a room by myself—melancholy—and no child to converse withal, so I was inclined by my genius, from my earliest years, to the love of antiquity. When a boy, long before I went to school, I did ever love to converse with old men, as living histories. I was always enquiring of my grandfather of the old time. I was born at Easton Pierce in the county of Wiltshire of long-living, healthy kindred, on March 12th—St. Gregory's Day—Anno Domini 1626, about sun-rising, being very weak and so like to die that I was christened before morning prayer. I think I have heard my mother say that I had an ague shortly after I was born, and about three or four years old, I had a grievous ague. I can remember it. Sickness of vomiting, the belly-ache, pain in the side, for twelve hours every fortnight for several years, then about monthly, then quarterly, and then at last once in half a year. About twelve it ceased altogether, but this sickness nipped my strength in the bud.

(AUBREY *rises, picks up sleeveless gown with fur hem and struggles into it.*)

A gentlewoman of my acquaintance had a beloved daughter, who had long been ill and received no benefit from her physicians. She dreamed that if she gave her daughter a drench of yew pounded, she would recover. The mother gave her daughter the drench, and it killed her, whereupon she grew quite distracted. Her chamber maid, to humour her, and to mitigate her grief, said, surely that could not kill her, she would adventure to drink the same herself. She did so, and it killed her also. This was about the year 1670 or 1671. I knew the family.

(AUBREY *goes to kitchen area, takes milk jug, sniffs, pours milk into a saucepan and puts it on the fire to heat.*)
Many people nowadays fear the physician more than the disease. (*Sits beside fire on stool*) A gent with a red ugly pumpled face came to the illustrious Doctor Butler for a cure. Said the doctor: "I must hang you"—so presently he had a device made ready to hang him from a beam, and when he was e'en almost dead, he cut the veins that fed these pumples and let out the black ugly blood and cured him.
(*Rises to kitchen table, collects brown bread on pewter plate, returns with it to table near the fire.*)
The Doctor, lying at the Savoy in London next the waterside where there was a balcony looked into the Thames, a patient came to him that was grievously tormented with an ague. The doctor discoursed with his patient, a gent, on the balcony when, on a signal, two or three lusty fellows came behind the gentleman and threw him a matter of twenty feet into the Thames. This surprise absolutely cured him. I would rather take physic from an old woman that had been at sick people's bedsides than from the most learned physician. (*Sits in front of fire*) Old Mistress Markey told me, to cure a child of the Thrush—take a living frog, and hold it in a cloth that it does not go down the child's mouth, and put the head into the child's mouth till it be dead. The frog. And then, take another frog. And so on.
(*Imitating the action throughout,* AUBREY *throws the imaginary dead frog over his shoulder, and is about to repeat the action a third time when he interrupts himself.*)
But, to Dr. Will Butler—he was a man of great moods, a humorist.
(*While relating the following anecdote,* AUBREY *peers to see how well his milk-pan is boiling, and takes it off the fire.*)
A serving man brought his master's water to Doctor Butler, who, being in his study, would not be spoken with. After much fruitless importunity the man told the doctor he was resolved he should see his master's water, he would not be turned away, and threw it on the doctor's head. This

humour so pleased the Doctor, he went to the gentleman and cured him.

(*Unconsciously,* AUBREY *accompanies the story he has just related to his own actions with the saucepan of milk, and not realising anything, throws the milk all over the floor. Puzzled, he looks at the empty pan, and without being aware of having spilt the milk, goes, as at first, to the kitchen table and pours out some more. Returns and places the pan gingerly on fire. Then, seeing the milk spilt all over the floor in front of him, looks up at the roof to see where it might have come from.*)

A Frenchman came one time to Cambridge, purposely to see the Doctor, whom he made stay for him in his gallery, and then he came out to him in an old blue gown. The French gentleman makes him two or three very low bows to the ground. Dr. Butler whips his leg over his head, and away he goes into his chamber and would not speak with him.

(*Imitating the action to the words,* AUBREY *totters backwards on to the chest, and strains his back in the process.*)

Ah. . . . Sir Jonas Moore . . . sciatica. He cured it by boiling his buttock.

(AUBREY'*s eye is taken by a mysterious earthenware dish on top of the gallery steps, with a cloth and small jar within it. He takes this carefully on to the main table, where everybody can see what he is doing. Ceremoniously, he reveals porringer, seeds and cloth, and demonstrates in actions what he relates in speech.*)

My honoured friend, Sir Edmund Wyld, (who had the misfortune to kill a man in 1664) one evening, just before we sat down to dinner, sowed in an earthen porringer of prepared earth, seeds of parsley. This porringer was covered with a dark cloth, and by the time we had ended dinner, nineteen or twenty young plants sprang visibly up, ready for cutting. This porringer has been in my possession ever since.

(AUBREY *goes over to fireside stool, as the Night-Watchman walks under the window calling the hour.* AUBREY *puts on a well worn pair of slippers.*)

NIGHT-WATCHMAN: God give you good-morning, my masters, past eight o'clock and a fair morning.

AUBREY: When I was a small boy, before the Civil Wars, the fashion was for old women and maids to tell fabulous stories, night-times, of spirits and walking ghosts: the old country people would talk much of fairies. They swept up the hearth clean at night, and set their shoes by the fire, and many times should find a threepence in one of them in the morning. Old Mistress Markey told me her mother had as much money from the fairies as made her a little silver cup of thirty shillings in value. When I was a boy, before the Civil Wars, I heard them tell that in the old time, they used to put a penny in the dead person's mouth to give to St. Peter and at Christmas, after prayer, in the country churches, they used to dance and sing, for in the infancy of the Christian religion, it was the fashion to plough, as they say, with the heifer of the Gentiles, and turn the pagan feast of Saturnalia into Christmas. 'Twas prudently done, to turn the image of Jupiter with his thunderbolts to Christ crucified, and Venus and Cupid into the Madonna and her Babe. It was quite the custom then for some people that were more than ordinary curious to sit all night in their church porch on Midsummer eve, to watch the apparitions of those that should die in the parish that year, come and knock at the door. When the wars came, the phantoms vanished. Now children fear no such things—and yet, not twenty years ago, not far from Cyrencester, there appeared an apparition. Mr. Lilly believes it was a fairy, but being demanded whether a good spirit or a bad, it returned no answer, but disappeared with a curious perfume, and a most melodious twang. I remember, at Oxford, the custom was——

(*Milk boils over and disrupts* AUBREY'*s wistful mood.*)

Well, the Civil Wars coming on have put all these "customs" quite out of fashion, and the divine arts of printing and gunpowder have frighted away Robin Goodfellow and the Fairies. Wars do not only extinguish

religion, but superstition also—and nothing disperses phantoms more readily than gunpowder.
(AUBREY *takes the saucepan of boiling milk and pours it on to the plate of brown bread, already on the table. Sits in favourite armchair before the fire. Sopping up the milk in bread, dribbling frequently,* AUBREY *continues talking, attempting to eat at the same time.*)
What was I best fitted to do? Truly nothing. Only umbrages. At eight I was a kind of engineer, and then I fell to drawing, and at nine, to colours. If I were ever to be good for anything, it would have been a painter. My greatest delight was to be continually with the joiners and masons and carpenters. Lamented much with myself not to have lived in a city . . . Bristowe . . . where I might have had access to watchmakers and locksmiths. It would have tempted me to have been a botanist had I had leisure. My idea very clear, like a mirror, pure crystal water. Apprehension enough—but memory not tenacious. Sir Edward Leech says sloth and carelessness are equal to all other vices. Though zeal for learning, but bred ignorant at Easton Pierce under several dull, ignorant house-teachers. Sent to Blandford School in Dorset under Mr. William Sutton B.D., who was ill-natured. Blandford was the most eminent school for the education of gentlemen in the West of England. I was like a bird that had got out of his cage amongst the free citizens of the air. I had a fine little horse, and commonly rode. But the boys mocked and abused me. I had a fine spinning top which was stolen from me. Eight years old before I knew what theft was. The grand-nephews of the great Sir Walter Raleigh were my schoolfellows, boisterous blades with excellent tuneable voices, and played their parts well on the viol. Ingeniose. But all proud and quarrelsome. I was fain to make friendship with a strong boy as a line to protection. I very well remember that excessive whipping when I was a little child did make a convulsive pain in my tender brain, and which doubtless did me a great deal of hurt. The tedious effects of grammar and the tyrannical beating of children,

from which many tender spirits do never recover has set me to compose an Idea of the Education of a young Gentleman from the age of nine or ten years 'till seventeen or eighteen:

(AUBREY *rises and goes over to the long table near the window, where his manuscripts are laid out. After a quick search, he discovers the papers he is looking for, and takes them to the desk.*)

"Youth should be indulged as to all lawful pleasures." 'Tis a very ill thing to cross children, it makes them ill-natured. "A school should be the house of play and pleasure, and not fear and bondage." I therefore decide never to overcloud their tender memories, but let them, when they begin to weary, turn the globes and play with them. "Scholars should not be beaten about the head." But to discourage the most serious naughtiness, thumbscrews would have to be employed. If I saw a young gentleman in an alehouse, I would be very severe with him —but if I caught him in a tavern, I would chide him mildly. It is observed that those children who are too severely prohibited to drink wine do generally prove drunkards. Besides which, wine is acknowledged to be a good medicine against the worms. "No scholar to rise too early", because it checks their perspiration, and so dulls them: it stints their growth. And so, in the garden, a noble basin to learn the art of swimming, and in the warm weather, to wash themselves. Neither the Provost nor the Ushers to marry, for if they did their daughters would debauch the young gents, not to say worse, to become their wives, for 'tis well known, he that looseth his maidenhead with a bare-legged wench, will never run after a silk-stocking. I intend to educate free ten Swiss, or Dutch, or Scottish boys. The French boys will be naught. Their minds do chiefly run on the propagation of their race.

(AUBREY *leaves the writing desk and returns to the other side of the table.*)

By experience I have found the only time of learning is from nine to sixteen. After that, Cupid begins to tyrannize.

Master* Hobbes told me that George, the Second Duke of Buckingham, when he was about twenty years old, had at Paris desired Mr. Hobbes to read Geometry to him. His Grace had great "natural parts", and quickness of wit. Master Hobbes read, and his Grace did not apprehend him, which Master Hobbes wondered at. At last, he observed that his Grace was at mastrupation. (*Pause*) He had his hand in his codpiece. Oh, that is a very improper age, for that reason—(*Pause*)—for learning.
(AUBREY, *collecting his stick from the centre table, takes milk jug to kitchen.*)
My school would have nothing of terror to frighten youths from the love of learning. I would have no such thing as the turning up of bare buttocks for pedants to exercise their cruel lusts. And yet, at Oxford, and I *do* believe the like at Cambridge, the rod was frequently used by the tutors and deans on their pupils, until they were Bachelours of Arts. One doctor I knew right well—Dr. Gill—a very ingeniose person, as may appear by his writings, but notwithstanding he had moods and humours and whippings fits. This Dr. Gill whipped Sir John Duncomb, who was a Colonel of the Dragoons, for pissing against the wall. Another of his pupils, Dr. Triplett of Westminster, came back to visit his old Master, and he whipped him. The Doctor was so afrighted that he did beshitt himself most fearfully. (*Goes back to sit in armchair*) And Dr. Triplett became most severe. I'll tell you a story of our old friend, George Ent, who went to school to him. Dr. Triplett was a great lover of honey. The Doctor was in his study: the boy takes confidence to approach with his "Quaeso, praeceptor, da mihi mel"—Please, sir, give me some honey—G. Ent was sneaking behind. Quoth the Doctor: "You audacious rascal", and gives him a good cuff on the ear. "How dare you be thus impudent—who put you on?" The boy answers

* Although I have sought expert advice, it was not possible to ascertain whether *Mr.* as frequently written by Aubrey, was pronounced *Master* or *Mister*. For production purposes we decided upon *Master* simply because it sounded less modern. P.G.

whiningly: "G. Ent." The enraged doctor flies out of his study, he was a very strong man, and gives poor George a kick in the breeches, and made him fly down a flight of stairs to the landing, where his head first came to, and he was stunned. He shaled a tooth. 'Twas as well his neck was not broken. 'Twas a most cruel and inhumane act to use a poor child so. The next day the learned and grave Dr. Ent took his son away, and placed him with Mr. Radford, an honest, sequestered fellow of Trinity College, Oxford.

(AUBREY *gets up from the armchair, goes over to his bed, bends down and pulls out a pewter chamber-pot, which he takes behind the far side of the four-poster, modestly pulling the curtain behind him.*)

To my great joy I was entered at Trinity College, as a gentleman commoner in my seventeenth year. Here I enjoyed the greatest felicity of my life, was made much of by my Fellows, had their learned conversation, looked on books, music.

(*From behind the drawn curtain of the bed comes an unmistakeable sound. A few moments later,* AUBREY *emerges with the chamber-pot discreetly covered with an elegant cloth, trimmed with lace.*)

"Ingeniose youths, as rosebuds, imbibe the morning dew."

(AUBREY *walks over to the window cautiously looks out to make sure nobody is walking underneath, and tips the contents of the chamber out. After covering once more the pewter chamber with the cloth, he replaces it beneath the four-poster, and unconcernedly wipes his hands on the curtains of the bed. Sniffing an orange-pomander to refresh himself, he returns to the armchair in front of the fire.*)

When I was at Trinity College, Doctor Ralph Kettell was then President, a very tall, well-grown man, a good deal above eighty. He had a terrible gigantic aspect, with sharp eyes. He was irreconcilable to long hair; called them hairy scalps. When he observed the scholars' hair longer than ordinary, especially if they were scholars of the house, he would bring a pair of scissors in his muff, which he commonly wore, and woe be to them that sat on the outside of the table. I remember he cut Mr. Radford's hair with the knife that chips the bread on the Buttery hatch. And then he sang: "And was not Grim the Collier finely trimmed! Tonedi, Tonedi." He spake in a thin, shrill, high treble. When he scolded at the idle young boys of his College, he called them: Turds, Tarrarags, Rascal-Jacks, Blind-sinks, Scobber-lotchers. To make you merry, I'll tell you a story that Dr. Henry Birkett told us t'other day at his cousin Mariet's. Mistress Howe of Grendon, sent him a present of Hippocras and some fine cheese cakes, by a plain country-fellow, her servant. The Doctor tastes the wine: "What" said he, "didst thou take this drink out of a ditch?" And when he saw the cheese cakes—"What have we here, Crinkum Crankum?" The poor fellow stared at him. . . ! Crinkum-Crankum! I cannot forget a story that Robert Skinner told me. One Master Isham, a gentleman-commoner, died of the smallpox. He was a very fine and well-beloved gentleman, and several of the Fellows would have preached his funeral sermon, but Dr. Kettell would not permit it, but would do it himself. Which the Fellows were very sorry for. When he came to the Panegyric, sayd he: "He was the finest sweet young gentleman; it did my heart good to see him walk along the Quadrangle. We have an old proverb that 'Hungry dogs will eat dirty puddings', but I must needs say for this young gentleman that he always loved sweet things." And there was an end. The Fellows knew he would make a ridiculous piece of work of it. 'Tis probable this venerable doctor might have lived some years longer, and finished his Century, had not those Civil Wars come on: which much grieved him, that was wont to be absolute in the college, to be affronted and disrespected by rude soldiers. I remember being at a rhetoric lecture in the hall, and a foot-soldier came in and brake his hour glass.

Our College Grove was the Daphne for the ladies and their gallants to walk about in, and many times my lady Isabella Thynne, who lay at Balliol College, would make her entry with a lute played before her. She was most beautiful, most humble, charitable, but she could not subdue one thing. She and her great friend, Mistress Fenshawe, who lay at our College, were wont to come to chapel in the mornings, half dressed, like angels—(*pause*) loose women.

The dissoluteness of the times, as I have said, grieving the good old Doctor, his days were shortened, and he dyed, and was buried at Garsington. How he would have ranted and beat-up his Kettel drum, if he could have seen such luxury in the College as there is now! Tempora Mutantur. Tempora Mutantur.

STREET CRY: New oysters—new Wallfleet oysters—
New mussels—new lilywhite mussels—
New mackerel—new mackerel—new mackerel—
new.

(AUBREY *goes down to the grate, throws on logs, and pokes fire, leaving the poker to heat in the glowing coals.*)

In 1642, war thundered, and as a clear sky is sometimes suddenly over-stretched with dismal cloud and thunder, so was the serene peace by the Civil Wars. Churches were pulled down to the ground, tuneable bells were converted into ordinance, and many houses were burnt. With much ado, I got my father to let me to my beloved Oxford again, then a garrison for the King. When I was a Freshman, I was wont to go to Christ Church to see King Charles the First at supper. I once heard him say that as he was hawking in Scotland, he rode into a Quarry and found a covey of partridges falling upon the hawk. I remember this expression, and I will swear upon the book 'tis true. When I came to my chamber, I told this story to my tutor. Says he: That covey was Parliament.

(AUBREY *rises, goes to table for stick.*)

With several of the King's party I grew acquainted, and many of them I knew before. Captain Carlo Fantom, a Croat. Spake thirteen languages: he was very quarrelsome and a very great ravisher. He left the Parliament party to join the King at Oxford, where he was hanged—for ravishing. Said he: I care not for your cause. I come to fight for your half-crown and your handsome women. The Earl of Essex held this Captain Fantom in high esteem, and twice saved him from being hanged for ravishing—once at Winchester, and a second time at St. Albans. He was content not only to do it himself, but he would make his soldiers do it too. And he would stand by, and look on. Oh, an admirable horse-officer, and a very great . . . ravisher.

No, I love not to debauch.

(*He goes to the table and collects a jug of wine, and a pewter tankard, and returns to the stool. From the interior of the house somewhere, a lute-player tunes and practices. He plays "Farewell", a Fancy by Dowland. This same melody is repeated several times throughout the play.*)

Oh, the Court were neat enough and gay in their apparel, yet they were very nasty and beastly, leaving at their departure from Oxford their excrements in every corner; in coal-houses, cellars, in chimneys and studys. Vain, empty and careless, rude, rough, whore-mongers.

(AUBREY *plunges the red-hot poker into his tankard to mull his own claret.*)

But King Charles was the pattern of courtesy. Till his time, the Court itself was unpolished and unmannered.

(*For a moment he listens to the faint chords of the lute, then makes a sour face at his claret.*)

My stomach is so tender, I cannot drink claret without sugar, or I will disgorge.

(AUBREY *goes to kitchen table, and stirs several spoonfuls of brown sugar in his tankard, then returns to seat.*)

I well remember it was frequently and soberly affirmed by officers of the army that the body of Charles the First was privately put into the sand about Whitehall. And the coffin that was carried to Windsor and laid in King Henry the Eighth's vault was filled with rubbish and brickbats.

(*After listening for a second or two longer to the lute-melody,* AUBREY *places his tankard by the fire and carefully makes his way up to the library, the corner nearest the window, where he looks for, and eventually finds the book he is referring to.*)

In December, 1648, King Charles the First, being in great trouble and a prisoner at Carisbrooke, about to be brought to London to his trial, Mr. Abraham Cowley, the poet, went to wait on the Prince of Wales, being then at Paris, and in profound sorrow for his father. His Highness asked him whether he would play at cards to divert his sad thoughts. Mr. Cowley replied, he did not care to play at cards, but if his Highness pleased, he would read some lines from Vergil's Aeneid. Mr. Cowley always had a Vergil in his pocket. The Prince understood not Latin well, and desired Mr. Cowley to translate the verses, which he did, admirably well, and Mr. George Ent, who lived in his house in the Great Plague of 1665, shewed me Mr. Cowley's own handwriting:

(AUBREY *reverently unfolds leaf of paper, which he finds stored in the back binding of the book.*)

By a bold people's stubborn arms oppressed,
Forced to forsake the land he once possessed,
Torn from his dearest son, let him in vain
Seek help, and see his friends unjustly slain.
Let him to base unequal terms submit,
In hope to save his crown, yet lose both it
And life at once, untimely let him die,
And on an open stage unburied lie.

(*Absorbed in the book, which he has taken over to the light next to the window* AUBREY, *reads on quietly to himself, turning the page. Finally, he breaks into his own reverie.*)

Now as to the last part, Mr. Fabian Philips assures me that the King's coffin did cost but six shillings. A plain deal coffin.

(AUBREY *leans forward on the balustrade of the gallery.*)

Oh, the new doctrine was very taking, and the more because there was no possibility of the King's return, but the greatest part of the parliament men were cursed tyrants and in love with their power, they ground anyone they owed ill will, to powder. Henry Marten, one of the late

King's judges, was a great lover of pretty girls, and King Charles 1st had a complaint against him for his wenching. The King espied him in Hyde Park one time, and said aloud: "Let that rascal be gone out of the park, that whore-master. . . ." That sarcasm raised up the whole county of Berkshire against the King. Henry Marten was as far from a Puritan as light from darkness, but he stored up that bitterness deep in his heart. His stature was middling, his habit moderate, his face *not* good. His company was incomparable, but he would be drunk too soon. His speeches in the House of Commons were not long, but wondrous poignant and witty. Oliver Cromwell once called him scoffingly *Sir* Harry Marten. Henry rises and bows: "I thank your Majesty. I always thought when you were King, I should be knighted." Oliver wondered at his impudence. But for the most part the parliament men were hated by the army and the country they represented, and their name and memory stinks. 'Twas worse than tyranny. I remember my friend Wenceslas Hollar, the engraver, told me that when he first came into England, which was a serene time of peace, the people—both poor and rich—did look cheerfully. But at his return, he found the countenances of the people all changed, melancholy, spiteful, as if bewitched.

(AUBREY *leaves the gallery of his library, and walks down to sit in the centre of the staircase, on one of the bottom steps.*)

In St. Edmund's Church at Salisbury were curious painted-glass windows of such exquisite work—I think it was in the chancel—that the Spanish Ambassador did offer some hundreds of pounds for it. In one of the windows was the picture of God the Father, painted, as the fashion then was, very like an old man. Now there is not a piece of glass painting left, the very bars taken out of the windows, the doors and paving gone, and the Font used to make a trough. Modern Puritan zeal had been reforming thereabouts. Such was the fanatic rage of the late times, that at Croydon in Surrey, a man was hired for half a crown a day, to break the painted-glass church windows.

(AUBREY *gets up from the stairs and walks over to the window, and looks out. From the street come noises of the midday market. This later changes into the ringing of peals of London bells. As* AUBREY *returns from the windows, during the speech about the Restoration, the sun pours through the windows, and reaches its brightest point. All the shadowy corners of the room are finally revealed in a clear winter light.*)

Long before these days, Colonel Massey and Thomas Mariett esquire, held correspondence with his Majesty Charles 2nd, who wrote them letters with his own hand, which I have seen. Every night, I had an account of these transactions which like a sot as I was, I did not while fresh in my memory commit to writing, but I remember in the main, that the generality of the City and the country were for restoring the King. Threadneedle Street was all day long, and late at night so crammed with multitudes crying out: "A free Parliament, a free Parliament," that the air rang.

One evening General Monk came out on horseback. They were so violent he was almost afraid for himself, and so, to satisfy them, cried out "Pray be quiet" as they used to do to children, "ye shall have a free Parliament"—Immediately a loud holla, and shout—This about seven, or rather eight, as I remember, at night—and all the bells in the city ringing, and the whole city looking as if it had been aflame by the bonfires, which were prodigiously great and ran like a train of gunpowder and I saw balconies and roofs that began to kindle. They made little gibbets in the streets, and roasted rumps of mutton (and I saw some very good rumps of beef). The people drank healths to the King in the streets by the bonfires, even on their knees, and, as the morn grows lighter and lighter, more glorious till it was perfect day, so it was with the joy of the people. Maypoles —which in the hypocritical times, 'twas a sin to set up, were now set up in every cross-way, and at the Strand near Drury Lane was the most prodigious maypole that perhaps was ever seen. This humour ran to Salisbury, where there was like joy, and so to Broadchalk, where they made a great bonfire on the hill, from hence to Blandford, and to Shaftesbury, and so to Land's End and so all over England. King Charles 2nd was crowned at the very conjunction of the Sun and Mercury—the cannons and thunder played together, and it lightened extremely.

(AUBREY *supports himself on his stick and looks wearily at his unfinished manuscripts, disordered in piles on the long table in front of him. The peal of bells slowly merges into the natural sounds of activity in the street outside, occasional street-criers, carriages, or horses trotting by.*)

Ah, God bless me and comfort me, that I may but live to finish and publish my papers.

For it hath pleased God to raise up a poor worm to do His Majesty humble service. I have made a Book of Lives. 'Twill be a pretty thing, for I spare neither friend nor foe, but am a religious tell-truth. Doctor Wallis, Keeper of the Archives in Oxford, tells me, I am too minute; but a hundred years hence, this minuteness will be grateful. For 'tis a task that I never thought to have undertaken till it was imposed upon me, by reason of my general acquaintance, having now lived the greater part of a century in the world, and having been much tumbled up and down in it, beside the modern advantage of coffee-houses. I here lay down to you the truth, and as near as I can, and as religiously as a penitent to his Confessor, nothing but the truth: the naked and plain truth, so bare that the very pudenda are not covered and many passages will raise a blush in a young virgin's cheeks.

(*Brushing away two or three small leaves which have blown through the open window on to his manuscripts,* AUBREY *turns away from the table, and selects precisely a volume of biography from a pile that lies on the top step of the gallery.*)

What uncertainty do we find in printed histories? Treading on the heels of truth, they dare not speak plain! Exempli gratia—"John Selden, jurist, quickly taken notice of for his learning—solicitor and steward to the Earl of Kent. One of the Assembly of Divines—one of the greatest critics of his time—eminent practiser at the bar." My saddler, who wrought many years with this family, told me—he got more by his prick than his practice. This solicitor and steward, was quickly taken notice of, not by the Earl of Kent, but by his Countess, who being an ingeniose woman and loving men would let him lie with her, and her husband knew it. After the Earl's death he married her, and he then did lie with Mistress Williamson, a lusty, bouncing woman, who robbed him on his death-bed. He never owned his marriage with the Countess of Kent till after her death, and he had a daughter, if not two, by another, and they did also talk of my lady's She-Blackamoor. "Great practiser." My saddler told me, he got more by his prick than by his practice.

(AUBREY *returns the book to the table, and after a final tidying of his manuscripts, moving them a few inches to the left, and then moving them back again, he returns to his favourite armchair by the fire. Taking a wooden bowl of quid-tobacco on to his lap, he draws out his personal knife and cuts the quid into small pieces.*)

'Tis a pity that such minutes had not been taken a hundred years since, for 'tis the greatest pleasure of an old man to renew acquaintance with his old and deceased friends. I remember a saying of General Lambert's, that "the best of men are but men of the best"—and you'll meet many examples in my rude and hasty collection.

TOWN-CRIER: Twelve o'clock . . twelve o'clock . . twelve o'clock.

AUBREY: These reminiscences are like fragments of a shipwreck, that after the revolution of so many years and governments have escaped the teeth of time and the hands of mistaken zeal. The retrieving of these forgotten things from oblivion in some way resembles the art of a conjuror, who makes those that have lain in their grave many hundreds of years, appear and walk. . . .

(*Imperceptibly,* AUBREY *drops off to sleep.*)

And to represent, as it were, to the eye, the places, the customs and fashions, of the old times. When I was a boy, before the Civil Wars, I heard old Sir Thomas Malet say that the great Sir Walter Raleigh, notwithstanding his conversation with the most learned and politest persons, yet he spake broad Devonshire to his dying day. Sir Walter was the first to introduce tobacco into England and into fashion, and I remember I heard old father Symonds say that Sir Walter took a pipe of tobacco a little before he went on the scaffold to settle his spirits, and that to his knowledge, he died with a lie in his mouth. . . . I have now forgot what 'twas. . . .

(AUBREY'*s head drops forward onto his chest. For a second he flickers into wakefulness, but his lids hang heavily and he sinks into a deeper sleep. The sun appears to hide behind a cloud, and the room is replaced with its former shadows. In the distance, the street-singer approaches.*)

STREET-SINGER: Her hair was black, her eyes were blue,
Her mouth as red as wine,
And he smiled to look upon her,
Did this sly, bold Reynardine. . . .

(*The singer fades away.* AUBREY *stays in his armchair, hands loosely clutching the tobacco-bowl, head bent forward in sleep.*)

End of Act One

ACT TWO

JOHN AUBREY *remains fast asleep in his armchair. The street-singer approaches. During the second verse of the song, the sun comes out from behind the cloud and floods the attic-room in bright light.*

SINGER: If bechance you'll look for me,
Perhaps you'll not repine,
But I'll be in my castle,
Enquire for Reynardine.

So light and dark she followed him,
His eyes did brightly shine,
And he led her over the mountains
Did this sly, bold Reynardine.

(*Next door the baby wakes with a cry, and in turn the child's squalling wakes* AUBREY.)

AUBREY: Ah, yes, Sir Walter Raleigh!

(*The mother sings her baby to sleep with a lullaby.*)

Sir Walter Raleigh was a tall, handsome and bold man, but his blemish was that he was damnable proud. He had a most remarkable aspect, an exceeding high forehead, long-faced, sour-lidded, a kind of piggy-eye. His beard turned up, naturally. He loved a wench well; and one time getting up one of the Maids of Honour up against a tree in a wood, she was something modest, and fearful of her Honour. "Sweet, Sir Walter" she cried, "sweet Sir Walter, what do you me ask? Will you undo me? Nay, sweet Sir Walter! Sweet Sir Walter! Sir Walter. . . !" At last, as the danger and pleasure at the same time grew higher, she cried in the ecstasy, "Swisser Swatter Swisser Swatter. . . ." She proved with child, and I doubt not but this Hero took care of them both. My old friend Sir James Harrington Esquire was an acquaintance of Sir Walter

Raleigh's. He told me that being invited to dinner with some great person, where his son was to go with him, Sir Walter said to his son: "Thou art such a quarrelsome, affronting creature, that I am ashamed to have·such a bear in my company." Master Walt promised his father he would behave himself. So, away they went, and young Master Walt was very demure at least until half dinner time. Then, says he: "I, this morning went to a Whore. I was very eager of her, kissed and embraced her, and went to enjoy her, when she thrust me from her, and vowed I should not, 'for', says she, 'your father lay with me but an hour ago.' " Sir Walter, being so strangely surprised and put out of countenance at so great a table, fetches his son a damned blow over the face. His son, rude as he was, would not strike his father, but strikes the face of the Gentleman that sat next to him and says: "Box about, 'twill come to my father anon." 'Tis now a common proverb.
(AUBREY *selects a spill from a mug near the fire and lights a dirty-stemmed clay-pipe.*)
Sir Walter was a person in every way, as King Charles the First says, of whom a Prince would be afraid of, rather than ashamed of. The time of his execution was contrived to be on my Lord Mayor's Day, that the Pageants and fine shows might draw away the people from beholding the tragedy of one of the gallantest worthies that ever England bred. A scaffold was erected in the old Palace yard, upon which, after 14 years stay of execution his head was struck off. Being asked which way he would lay himself on the block, as he stretched himself along it, he said: "So the heart be right, it is no matter which way the head lieth." Such abundance of blood issued from his veins, that showed he had stock of life enough to have continued many years, though now above three score years old. And this was the end of the great Sir Walter Raleigh. His nephews were my schoolfellows. They had excellent tuneable voices, and played their parts well on the viol, but all proud and quarrelsome.
(*Again the child next door starts crying.*)

Oh, Lord bless me . . . will this never cease?

(AUBREY *rises, goes over and beats with stick on the wall.*)

MOTHER: You stupid old fool in a tattered gown. . . .

AUBREY: This mother's shrill tongue and singing to the cradle are intolerable.

(AUBREY *still smoking, crosses over to manuscript-table to clear a space for his midday meal.*)

I knew a wealthy clothier of Milsham, Isaac Self, who died in the ninety second year of his age, leaving behind him a numerous offspring—videlicet: eighty and three in number. Eighty and three. Mistress Hine, the vicar's wife, a very able midwife, did tell a story which was confidently believed that about Westerly or Alderly, or thereabouts, in Gloucestershire, there were two children born in the grave. The said mistress Hine also told a story of a monstrous birth at Dorchester, first a son, now living and the heir, and afterwards for eight days together, every day another child. Some had heads and arms, and no lower parts; others had lower, but no upper-parts. One had two heads, the one opposite the other; about four o'clock in the afternoon, the same day, it was christened, by the name of Martha and Mary, having two very pretty faces, and lived till Friday next. She never had any child afterwards. While 'tis in my mind. . . One Ricketts of Newbury, a practitioner in physic, excellent at the curing of children with swollen heads and small legs: the disease being new and without a name, he being so famous for the cure of it, they called it Ricketts. And now 'tis such good sport to see how they vex their lexicons, and fetch it from the Greek *Raxis*, the back-bone. . . .

(AUBREY *knocks out the ashes of his pipe, and leaves it on a plate on the table. Suddenly his eye falls upon the porringer referred to in the previous Act. He crosses over to the centre table, with a great deal of ceremony.*)

As I told you before—Master Edmund Wyld, a gentleman of a most superior order, sowed seeds in the morning, to be cut for salad *at dinner*.

(*Sweeping aside the dark cloth with a flourish,* AUBREY

discovers the seeds haven't grown at all, and after a closer look, mumbling to himself remarks like 'a gentleman of a most superior order' or 'to be cut for salad at dinner?', *takes the porringer over to the light, and throws the earth out of the window. He places the porringer on the sill, and looks down at the street. A single bell from a nearby church chimes.*)
I wish these windows might face South and East. In my former estate at Broadchalk, the church possessed one of the prettiest ring of bells in Wiltshire—the river running near the churchyard meliorates the sound. By my parlour window grew a Bon-Christian pear tree against the wall and in the garden beyond, a warden-pear that reclines.
(*He turns away from the window.*)
The winter before the Great Plague was just such a mild winter as this. At Petersham, last year, a plague made so great a destruction there only survived four of the inhabitants. The small-pox too, in all great towns. The physicans cannot master it.
(AUBREY *gets restless and fidgety, and paces around the centre of the room.*)
And now the chit in the chamber below falls sick of the small-pox, and Mistress Byerley, my good hostess, is afraid—never having had them—and fat. I would fain lie at Master Kent's but he has two children both sick of the same disease. Well, where should I lie. . . ? I had the good fortune lately to be offered lodgings in an empty house, and thought to bring my manuscripts with me and there finish them. I could do it in a fortnight. But 'twas not to be.
(*He walks up the steps to his library, tapping on his way the nose of a small stuffed-bear cub, whom he addresses.*)
I lacked my Plinys and my Homers for quotations!
(*He drags over a step-ladder, and climbs up to the highest shelf on his book-case in search of a book of Seneca.*)
My good master, Doctor William Harvey, dictated to me what to see, what books to read, how to manage my studies. He bid me go to the fountainhead—read Aristotle, Cicero, and Seneca. He called the new-fangled metaphysicals, George Herbert and Dr. Donne, shit-

breeches.
(*He murmers to himself an extract from Seneca.*)
"Quis candidatus laboret: quis alienis: quis suis varibus pugnet: quis consulatum: quis Pompei . . . quis, quis, quis, quis. . . ."
Venerable Doctor Kettell was wont to say that Seneca writes as a boar does piss—by jerks—*scilicet.* Quis, quis, quis, quis!
(AUBREY *replaces the volume of Seneca, and comes down the ladder.*)
Doctor Ralph Kettell—oh, he was a very tall well-grown man. He was irreconcileable to long hair. He called them hairy-scalps, and many was the time . . . but methinks I have already acquainted you with Doctor Kettell's humours. . . ? Indeed I have. Crinkum-crankum!
(*He goes from the library, down the gallery-steps, over to the kitchen, where he collects a plate and knife and fork, and returns by the fire to examine a pheasant carcass, which he takes with him, and lays on the space prepared at the manuscript-table.*)
It was always my intention to describe the pleasant county of Wiltshire, but I never completed it, my age being too far spent for such undertakings. Now I am stormed by my chiefest friends to turn ecclesiastic, and truly, if I had a good parsonage of two to three hundred pounds a year, it would be a shrewd temptation. How should I look in a cassock? As I was coming one time out of All Souls, Oxford, the gape-abouts at the gate pointed at me and one said: "Romano-Catholicus". I doubt how strongly the Church of England stands. If it changes, what shall I do then? Faugh! the cassock stinks, it would be ridiculous.
(*Sitting at the table, he tears and chews at the carcass of the bird.*)
When I heard Robert Sanderson, Lord Bishop of Lincoln, I do remember he had no great memory. When I was a Freshman and heard him read the lecture, he was out in the Lord's prayer. When he was a student at Christchurch, it fell to his lot to preach the Passion sermon, and 'twas

said of him then in the University that our Saviour never suffered so much since his Crucifixion. All things are not possible to all men. Richard Corbet, Doctor of Divinity, Bishop of Oxford, was the son of a gardener at Twickenham. His conversation was extremely pleasant. Dr. Stubbins was one of his cronies, a jolly, fat Doctor. As Dr. Corbet and he were riding in Lob Lane in wet weather ('tis an extraordinary deep, dirty lane) the coach fell. And Dr. Corbet said that Dr. Stubbins was up to the elbows in mud, and he was up to the elbows in Dr. Stubbins. One time, as Dr. Corbet was confirming, the country people pressed in to see the ceremony. Said he: "Bear off there, or I'll confirm ye with my staff". Being about to lay his hand on the head of a very bald man, he turns to his chaplain, Lushington, and says: "Some dust, Lushington", to prevent his hand from slipping. This chaplain, Dr. Lushington, was a very learned man, and they loved one another. Sometimes the Bishop would take the key of his wine-cellar, and he and his chaplain would lock themselves in and be merry. First he lays down his Episcopal gown—"There lies the Bishop"— Next he lays down his Episcopal hat—"There lies the Doctor"—then 'twas "Here's to thee, Corbet"—and "Here's to thee, Lushington". His antagonist, Dr. Price, was made Dean of Hereford, a mighty, pontifical, proud man, and when he went about the Cathedral church in procession, he would not do it in the usual way, on foot, but rode on a mare, with a common-prayer book in his hands, reading. A stallion happened to break loose, and smelt the mare, and ran and leaped her, and held the Reverend Dean all the time so hard in his embraces, that he could not get off 'till the horse had done his business. I know not why but he would never ride in procession afterwards. The last words Dr. Corbet said were "Good night, Lushington".

(AUBREY *takes a sheaf of manuscript and a quill, and writes Corbet's last words in the corner. He has no sooner finished when the baby next door once again starts crying even more furiously than before.* AUBREY *goes the whole way over to the*

wall, stick upraised, but instead of banging changes his mind and makes the sign of benediction. As if miraculously, to AUBREY*'s evident amazement, the yelling ceases abruptly.* AUBREY *looks gratefully upwards.*)
We should glorify God in his works.
(*He returns to his manuscript-table to collect the plate of bones.*)
'Till about the year 1649, 'twas held a strange presumption for a man to attempt an innovation in learning, and to be more knowing than his neighbours or forefathers was held not to be good manners. And yet not to take notice of what is daily offered before our eyes is gross stupidity. I have discovered, if you let fall a stone into the water, immediately it makes a little circle, then another bigger without that, and so forth until it touches the bank, then it recoils in a little circle, which generates other bigger circles. So sounds move, by spheres, in the same manner—which, though obvious enough, I do not remember to have seen written in any book. I do remember Dr. William Harvey, who discovered the circulation of the blood . . . Prussy, prussy, prussy. . . .
(*Forgetting his train of thought,* AUBREY *picks up the plate which contains the carcass of pheasant, and making coaxing sounds, wanders into the centre alcove in quest of his cat: he calls it, whistles to it, disappears out of sight, sets down the food, returns to the steps, the cat follows him, he chivvies it back again, and finally returns to the room, announcing briefly, by way of explanation,* "*Crinkum Crankum*". *He goes over to the armchair and sits in front of the fire.*)
William Laud, A.B.C.
Archbishop of Canterbury. He was a great lover of cats, and was presented with some cyprus-cats, prussy-cats, which were sold at first for five pounds apiece. I well remember that the common English cat was white with some blueish piedness, a gallipot-blue. The race or breed of them are almost lost.
(AUBREY *picks several hot chestnuts out of the fire, peels and eats them with the aid of his pen-knife.*)

But to Doctor Harvey—I have heard him say that after his admirable discovery of the circulation of blood, he fell mightily in his practise, the physicians wrote books against him, and 'twas believed by the vulgar that he was crack-brained. Crack-brained! My old friend Doctor Harvey—I knew him right well. He made me sit by him two or three hours together in his meditating department, discoursing. I remember he kept a pretty young wench to wait on him, which I guess he made use of for warmth sake, as King David did. He was often troubled with the gout, and his way of cure was thus: he would sit with his legs bare, if it were a frost, on the leads of his house, put them into a pail of water 'till he was almost dead with cold, and betake himself to a stove, and so 'twas gone. He lies buried in a vault at Hempsted in Essex; he is lapt in lead, and on his breast in great letters: DR. WILLIAM HARVEY. I was at his funeral and helped carry him into the vault. When a learned man dies—what a great deal of learning dies with him. Sir William Petty told me that about 12 or 13, there happened to him the most remarkable accident of his life which was the foundation of all the rest of his greatness, but he did not tell me what 'twas. This Sir William Petty had a boy that whistled incomparably well. He after waited on a Lady, a widow of good fortune. Every night this boy was to whistle his lady asleep. At last she could hold out no longer, but bids her chamber-maid withdraw, bids him come to bed, sets him to work, and marries him the next day. This is certain true. Francis Bacon, Viscount St. Albans and illustrious Lord Chancellor, was a pederast. His Ganimedes and favourites took bribes, and three of his servants kept coaches and some kept race-horses. He had a delicate, lively, hazel eye; Dr. Harvey told me it was like the eye of a viper. His Dowager married her Gentleman Usher, Sir Thomas, I think, Underhill, whom she made deaf and blind with too much of Venus.

(AUBREY *goes up to the chest in the centre of the room, lifts off dusty books placed on it, and a coverlet, and pushes the chest down towards the edge of the room, stopping to*

regain his breath, and ending up by sitting on it.)
Thomas Goffe, the poet, his wife was not so kind. She pretended to fall in love with him, by hearing him preach. Upon which his oldest confident and friend, Tom Thimble, said to him: "Do not marry her: if thou dost, she will break thy heart." 'Twas not long before this snip-cheese, this cursed shrew made Master Thimble's prediction good, and when he died, the last words he spake were: "Oracle, oracle, Tom Thimble", and so gave up the ghost.
(AUBREY *kneels down behind the ancient treasure-chest, and taps it significantly.*)
Some of these curiosities are so exceeding old, that no books reach them.
(*The lid opens with a creaking sound. Within, stacked to the top, are all kinds of treasures. With great reverence* AUBREY *takes out a grotesque inhuman prehistoric skull, regards it with love, appears to be about to say something, then puts it down. Then he slowly unwraps the next object, which is protected by several layers of different kinds of cloth.*)
When Father Harcourt suffered at the stake at Tyburn, his bowells etc. thrown into the fire, a butcher's boy standing by, was resolved to have a piece of his kidney which was broiling in the fire. He burned his fingers, but he got it, and one Roydon, a brewer in Southwark bought it. The wonder is, 'tis now absolutely—(*tapping it*) petrified. 'Twas not so hard when he first had it—but being carried in the pocket hardened by degrees, like an agate polished. I much value it. I did see Christopher Love beheaded on Tower Hill, in a delicate clear day; about half an hour after his head was struck off, the clouds gathered blacker and blacker and terrible claps of thunder and tempest, as if the machine of the world had been dissolving. Some would take delight in killing men—'tis the best lechery in the world to see 'em suffer correction. Your London aldermen take great lechery to see poor wretches whipped at Bridewell, others drawn on a hurdle, hanged, their entrails taken out living, and burnt before their eyes—'Twas the ill-fate of Sir Everard Digby to suffer so in the gun powder plot.

(AUBREY *rises, still holding Father Harcourt's petrified kidney, now wrapped, and moves back towards the four-poster bed, where he places it beside Dame Venetia Stanley's bust.*)
When his heart was plucked out by the executioner, who cried: "Here is the heart of a traitor!", it is credibly reported that Sir Everard replied: "thou liest!". One of the handsomest men of his time—his eldest son was Sir Kenelm Digby, a gentleman absolute in all numbers. He was such a goodly person, gigantic and a great voice, that had he been dropped out of the clouds in any part of the world, he would have made himself respected. The Pope said he was mad. Sir Kenelm used to say that a handsome, lusty man that was discreet might make a virtuous wife out of a brothel-house, and he married, much against his mother's consent, that celebrated beauty and courtesan, Miss Venetia Stanley, whom the Earl of Dorset kept as concubine, and had children by. She had a most lovely and sweet-turned face, and delicate dark brown hair. Healthy, strong, good skin, well-proportioned, much inclining to be a bona roba . . . near altogether.
(*From within the lodging-house, again the lute-player tunes his instrument and plays the same air by John Dowland.*)
The colour of her cheeks was just that of a damask rose, which is neither too hot nor too pale. She died in her bed suddenly. Some suspected she was poisoned. When her head was opened, there was found but little brain, which her husband imputed to the drinking of viper-wine, to preserve her beauty.
(AUBREY *touches gently the outline of the bust, half-concealed behind a black veil of lace.*)
About 1675 or 6, as I was walking through Newgate Street I saw Dame Venetia's bust from off her tomb, standing at a stall at the Golden Cross, a brazier's shop. I perfectly remembered it, but the Great Fire of London had got off the gilding. How these curiosities would be forgot, did not such idle fellows as I am put them down. The young men are learned enough, but no antiquities. I intended to see the antiquities of Rome, and then to have returned and

married, but my mother—to my inexpressible grief—hindered this design, which was my ruin. 'Tis not consistent with a harmonical soul to be a woman-hater.

(*Rather dejected by the reflections he has just made on his solitary life,* AUBREY *listens to the notes of the lute, and walks slowly down towards the fire, beating time with his hand. The lute ends, and at the same instant,* AUBREY'*s good-humour returns, and in better spirits he continues.*)

Mistress Elizabeth Broughton came of an ancient family, and whether she was born at Cannon-Peon or no, I know not, but there it was she lost her maidenhead to a poor country fellow, then I believe handsome, but in 1660, a pitiful poor old weaver, clerk of the Parish. He had fine curled hair, but grey. She was a most exquisite beauty, and her price was very dear. Richard, Earl of Dorset, kept her, but whether before or after Venetia, I know not, but I guess before. At last she grew common and infamous and got the pox, of which she died. I remember an old song of those days, 'twas by way of a litany:

From the Watch at Twelve o'clock,
And from Bess Broughton's button Smock,
Libera nos, Domine.

Her father was of the Puritan party, and had a great gift in praying.

(AUBREY *lights wooden spill at the fire, and lights candles on table. From this moment, the room gradually grows darker, and the shadows slowly fill the corners and alcoves. As much as possible, the change of light should be imperceptible. The quality of the light is that of a typical winter's day in London, sharp and yellow at midday, and then slowly becoming orange-flushed, and a deep livid red just before dusk. The colours are emphasized on the kitchen-side of the room, especially the four-poster bed and the high-backed chair, so that the room has by the evening an almost golden glow, and the browns and reds of the setting are suffused in the same light, like a painting by Rembrandt.*)

TOWN-CRIER: If any man or woman can tell any tidings of a little maiden-child about the age of five and seven, this little child was lost between the Standard and the pissing-conduit. If any man can bring any news of her, let him come to the crier, and he shall have fourpence for his labour. . . .

(AUBREY *takes over a candle to his manuscripts during the cry, having left one already alight on the centre-table. He reaches the window and looks out, imitating the inflections of the Crier.*)

AUBREY: And that's more than she's worth . . . and God's blessing.

On the Bankside in London here, were two bear-gardens, a theatre known by the name of the Globe Playhouse, and, not far from this, the Asparagus Gardens and Pimlico Path, much used by the comedians of the time. "To walk in Pimlico!" It became proverbial for a man handsomely dressed.

(AUBREY *returns to the velvet-stool near the fire.*)

Did I ever tell you I met Master Beeston, who knew all the old English Poets: his father was Master of the Playhouse. He knew Beaumont and Fletcher, Sir William Davenant, and brave Ben Jonson. Now, Ben Jonson was a Warwickshire man. He killed Mr. Marlowe, the poet, on Bunhill, coming from the Green Curtain Playhouse. He had one eye lower than the other, and bigger, like Clun, the player—perhaps he begot Clun. I have heard my uncle Danvers say, who knew him, that Ben lived at Westminster, in the house under which you pass as you go out the churchyard into the old palace, where he died.

(AUBREY *takes up his tankard of claret, nurses it, stirs in more sugar and drinks.*)

He would many times exceed in drink, and canary was his beloved liquor. King James made him write against the Puritans—"A Grace" by Ben Jonson:

Our King and Queen the Lord-God bless,
The Paltzgrave and the Lady Bess,
And God bless every living thing
That lives and breathes and loves the King.

God bless the Council of Estate,
And Buckingham the fortunate.
God bless them all, and keep them safe:
And God bless me and God bless Ralph.

Now King James was mighty inquisitive to know who this Ralph was. Ben told him 'twas the drawer at the Swan Tavern by Charing Cross who drew him good canary. For this, His Majesty gave him an hundred pounds. So much for brave Ben, he usually took too much before he went to bed. He lies buried in the North aisle, with this inscription only on him, about 14 inches square.

O RARE BEN JONSON

After Ben's death, Sir William Davenant was made poet laureate in his place. He got a terrible clap of a black handsome wench that lay in Axe-yard, Westminster, which cost him his nose. His mother was a very beautiful woman. Master William Shakespeare was wont to go into Warwickshire once a year and did commonly in his journey, lie in Mistress Davenant's house, in Oxford, where he was exceedingly respected. Sir William Davenant was wont to say, when he was pleasant over a glass of wine that he wrote in the very spirit that did Shakespeare, and that he seemed contented enough to be thought his son. And Sir William would tell this story to his intimate friends in which his mother had a very light report, whereby she was called a whore. This William Shakespeare was born at Stratford super Avon, where his father was a butcher and I have been told by some of his neighbours he exercised his father's trade—and when he killed a calf he would do it in a high style and make a speech. Being naturally inclined to poetry and acting, he came to London, I guess about eighteen, and was an actor at one of the playhouses, and though I have enquired, I could never meet with any further account of him this way, than that the top of his performance was the ghost in his own "Hamlet".* Mr.

Aubrey remembers Shakespeare only as an indistinct and not very important figure, and has to reflect to recall Hamlet at all.

Williams, a gentleman farmer occupying Clopton House near Stratford super Avon said to me: "By God, I wish you'd arrived a little sooner. Why it isn't a fortnight since I destroyed several baskets full of letters and papers, in order to clear a small chamber for some young partridges which I wanted to bring up alive: and as to your William Shakespeare why, there were many bundles with his name wrote upon them. Why, it was in this fireplace, I made a roaring bonfire of them. . . ."

In my grandfather's days, the manuscripts flew about like butterflies, but in the late wars, a world of rare manuscripts perished. When I went to see Parson Stump out of curiosity to see his manuscripts that I knew as a boy, they were all lost and dispersed. His sons were gunners, and soldiers, and scoured their guns out with them. I know some nauseate these old manuscripts, but I confess I regard them as the most considerable pieces of antiquity I collect.

(AUBREY *leaves the stool and crosses to armchair, which he swivels round beside the open chest. He takes out a long astrological chart and studies it carefully. Deeply superstitious, he anxiously examines the figures of the Zodiac, clustered round a naked female body.*)

My life is more remarkable in an astrological aspect than for any advancement of learning. I see Mars threatens danger to me from falls. Well, I have twice been in danger of drowning, a terrible fit of the spleen in 1664, and piles at Orleans. Then the year I lay at Mistress Neve's, in great danger of being run through with a sword by William, Earl of Pembroke, then Lord Herbert. Herbert? Herbert?

(*Swings round in his chair to point out picture of fashionably dressed Elizabethan lady, hanging in shadowy alcove behind.*)

Ah, Mary Herbert, Countess of Pembroke. She was a very salacious woman, and she had a contrivance that in the spring of the year, when the stallions were to leap the mares, they were to be brought before a part of the house where she had a vidette, a hole to peep out at, to look on them and please herself with their sport. And then she would act the like sport herself with *her* stallions. She was the sister to Sir Phillip Sidney, whose fame will never die: and there was so great love between them that I have heard old gentlemen say that they lay together.

(AUBREY *bends down into the chest and brings out two parchment-sheets, which he places close to the candle-light to decipher. He reads painstakingly.*)

". . . In several parts of Oxfordshire, it is the custom for the maidservant to ask the man for ivy to dress the house, and if the man neglects to fetch in the ivy, the maid nails up a pair of his breeches to the gate in the yard. . . ." Faugh! This is mere whim-wham.

(*He crumples it up and chucks it on the floor.*)

"Abraham Wheloc . . . simple *man*?"

(AUBREY *ponders, as if trying to put a face to the description. Then the message comes through.*)

Ah, "Abraham Wheloc" . . . *simple* man.

(AUBREY *rubs his tired eyes beneath their spectacles.*)

My candle grows low. Ever since I came from Oxon., I have a mist in my eyes: vapours, I suppose, rising from the spleen. My doctor sayeth it will wear off, but I must forbear reading. Indeed I can hardly read a letter nowadays. A doctor I know says the cure for blindness is to drink the bath-water.

(*He bends down into the chest, and comes out holding a whalebone sprig, with a small rag tied to the end of it.*)

This phlegm-stick makes you vomit without pain. I had a young fellow that was my servant, used it incomparably, he would touch the bottom of his stomach with it. The inventor was Walter Rumsey. He was much troubled with the phlegm, and one winter, being at court at Ludlow, sitting by the fire, spitting and spawling, he took a fine tender sprig, tied a rag on the end, and put it down his throat to fetch up the phlegm, so. (AUBREY *goes to demonstrate, but funks it.*) I could never make it go down my throat, but for those that can, 'tis a most wonderful engine. If troubled with the wind, it cures you immediately, with a blast as when a bottle is unstopped.

(*Replaces phlegm-stick in chest, and brings out the lower-half*

of a jaw-bone.)
Jawbone of old Sir Thomas More, Lord Chancellor. Methinks 'tis strange that all this time his Lordship is not canonised, he merited highly of the Church. His country house was at Chelsea, from whence there is a most pleasing prospect of the Thames and fields beyond. In his book, Utopia, his law is that the young people are to see each other stark-naked before marriage. Sir William Roper came one morning, pretty early, to see my Lord, with a proposal to marry one of his daughters. My Lord's daughters were then both together abed in a truckle bed in their father's chamber, asleep. He carries Sir William into the chamber and takes the sheet by the corner and suddenly whips it off. They lay on their backs with their smocks as high up as their arm-pits. This awakened them, and immediately they turned on their bellies. Quoth Roper—"I have seen both sides," and so gave a pat on the buttock he made a choice of, saying: "Thou art mine." Here was all the trouble of the wooing. I remember Dr. Corbet put a pretty trick on Doctor Fell to let him take a journey to London when he had already. . . . No, I have forgot the story . . . (*laughs to himself*) I have seen both sides. . . . (*Sudden depression*) God bless me, this searching after antiquities is a wearisome task—and yet methinks I am carried on by a kind of divine prompting.
(*Painfully he gets up, and helped along by his stick, walks across to the window, giving the porringer of miraculous seeds a final surreptitious look.*)
No one else cares for it hereabouts, they rather make a scorn of it: and yet I can affirm I have brought some things from utter darkness into a thin mist.
(*Ready to draw curtain across window,* AUBREY *has a last look at the streets of London.*)
If I die in London, as 'tis most likely, shall I be buried in St. Martin's, near the door, like a poor penitent? Or else, under the brick wall in the Fanatics Churchyard, with old Ned Bagshawe. Our bones never lie quiet in consecrated ground in London, for once every ten years the earth is

carried to the dung-wharf.

(*Perkily repeating the doggerel to himself, addressing the first and second lines to his favourite stuffed bear,* AUBREY *trots up the stairs to the gallery, to put away a book which he collects from the table. Then he goes over to the last uncurtained window and prepares to pull the blind across it.*)

Thus youth and age and all things pass away,
Thy turn is now as his was yesterday,
Tomorrow shall another take thy room,
And next day, he a prey for worms become.
And o'er your dusty bones shall others tread,
As you now walk and trample on the dead.
'Till neither stone nor memory appear,
That ever you had birth or being here.

(*Just at the end of the poem, the actual weight of what he is saying comes home to him, and again, there is a moment of despondency as he surveys the cluttered room, full of useless curiosities, and the table piled high with uncatalogued manuscripts.*)

'Tis a pity these papers should be buried in oblivion.

(*His whole mood alters as soon as he recalls another anecdote, and he comes to the centre of the gallery, in front of the main book-case.*)

Dame Olave Sherington, being in love with John Talbot, a younger brother of the Earl of Shrewsbury, and her father not consenting that she should marry him, discoursed with him one night from the battlements of the Abbey-church. Said she: "I will leap down to you." Her sweetheart replied: "And I will catch you," —never dreaming she would have done it. She leaped down and the wind, which was then high, came under her coats, and did something break the fall. Mr. Talbot caught her in his arms, but she struck him dead. She cried out for help, and he was with difficulty brought to life again. Her father told her, since she had made such a leap she should e'en marry him. She was my honoured friend. About 1651, being about an hundred years old, she died.

(*He comes down the stairs, and collects the candle from the manuscript-table.*)

My poor old friend, Sir James Harrington, he would discourage rationally enough, but he grew to have a fancy that his perspiration turned to flies, or bees. He had a versatile timber-house turned towards the sun, and would sit in it. Then he would have his foxtails there, to chase away and massacre all the flies and bees, that were to be found. A quarter of an hour after, perhaps, a fly or two, or more, might be drawn out of the lurking holes by the warmth. And then he would cry out: "Do not you see that these apparently come from me?" 'Twas the strangest sort of madness that ever I found in any one; talk of anything else, he would be very ingeniose and pleasant.

STREET-CRIER: Lanthorns and candle-light, hang out maid for all the night—Lanthorns and candle-light. . . .

(AUBREY *comes behind table, pulling back bed-covers as he passes the four-poster, sets candle on table together with his stick, and makes up fire for the night.*)

AUBREY: Henry Nevill Esquire never forsook him to his dying day. Though near a whole year before he died his memory and discourse were taken away, yet this gentleman paid his visits as duly and respectfully as when his friend was in the prime of his understanding. A true friend.

(*He warms the bed with the warming-pan. Blows out candle on the centre table, and lights the candle on the sideboard with a taper from the fire. He sits on the tall chair below the four-poster. The only light comes now from the candle beside him.*)

Nowadays surliness and inurbanity are too common in England. The present Earl of Pembroke has at Wilton, 52 mastiffs, 30 greyhounds, some bears and a lion and a matter of 60 servants more bestial than they. A better instance of a squeamish and dis-obliging fellow cannot be found than in Gwyn, the Earl of Oxford's secretary—he cuts some sour faces enough that would turn the milk in a fair lady's breast. This Earl of Oxford, Edward de Vere, making of his low obeisance to Queen Elizabeth, happened to let a fart, at which he was so abashed and ashamed that he went to travel, seven years. On his return the Queen welcomed him home, and said, "My Lord, we have forgot the Fart". The nobility and gentry were damnable proud and insolent in those days. Old Sir Henry Lee of Ditchley, Knight of the Garter, a gentleman of good estate, a bastard son of Henry the Eighth, christened all his children Harry's. He never married, but kept women to read to him when he was abed. One of his readers was Parson Jones's wife, of Wootton. I have heard her daughter, who had no more wit, say what a brave reader her mother was, and how Sir Harry's Worship much delighted to hear her. But his dearest dear was Mistress Anne Vavasour. He erected a noble altar monument of marble, whereon his effigies lay in armour, and at his feet the effigy of his mistress, Mistress Anne Vavasour. Which occasioned these verses:

Here lies the good old knight Sir Harry,
Who loved well, but would not marry.
While he lived and had his feeling,
She did lie and he was kneeling,
Now he's dead and cannot feel,
He doth lie and she doth kneel.

(*The lute-player from within plays the Dowland melody.* AUBREY *listens for a moment, before resuming his narrative.*)

I remember, when I was a little boy, before the Civil Wars, an old raven did build her nest on the church leads, between the tower and the steeple. The oldest people's grandfathers did never remember but that this raven yearly made her nest there. And in the late Civil Wars, the soldiers killed her. I am sorry for the tragical end of this old Church-bird that lived through so many changes of government and years and religion.

(*The lute continues its poignant melody.* AUBREY *listens, and, suddenly vexed, taps with his knuckles on the arm of the chair. The music ceases.*)

Ah, the misery of old age—surely the day of one's death must be counted among one's happiest. Yesterday, I saw Mr. Rushworth. He hath quite lost his memory with drinking brandy, remembering nothing. His landlady wiped his nose like a child. Eighty-three, onwards to eighty-four. He had forgot his children.

The rose withers, the blossom blasteth,
The flower fades, the morning hasteth,
The sun sets, the shadow flies,
The gourd consumes, and man he dies.

(*Now the room is in complete darkness, apart from a few shafts of moonlight that fall on the bookshelves. The candle flickers.*)

TOWN-CRIER: Good gracious people, for the Lord's sake, pity the poor prisoners, who lie cold and comfortless night and day in deep misery.

AUBREY: Amen, amen to that. Gideon de Laune, apothecary to Mary the Queen Mother, a very wise man, now decrepit with gout, a place for him in the chimney corner. Slighted, so Sir William Davenant tells me, not only by his daughter-in-law, but by the cook and the maid. And he was master of his own estate. Alas, O God's will, it was not so in Queen Elizabeth's time. Then youth bare respect to old age. Then the elders of the parish sat and beheld the pastimes of the young men as wrestling, shooting at Butts, bowling and dancing. All this is now lost; and pride, whoring, wantoness and drunkenness. Their servants, like clowns too, like drunkards too. Breeches of one sort, doublet of another, drabbled with the tears of the tankard and greasy. I foresaw and foretold all the late changes, and now easily foresee what will follow after. You see in me the ruins of time. The day is almost at an end with me, and truly I am glad of it. I desire not to live in this corrupt age. Alas, O God's will, it was not so in Queen Elizabeth's time.

(AUBREY*'s head falls forward. The* TOWN-CRIER *approaches and fades into the distance again.*)

TOWN-CRIER: Give ear to the clock, look well to your lock, and your fire, and your light, and God give you goodnight. Twelve o'clock . . . twelve o'clock . . . twelve o'clock.

(*In the next chamber the child wakes and cries lustily, but* AUBREY *remains still. The candle goes out.*)

STREET-SINGER: Light and dark she followed him,
His eyes did brightly shine,
And he led her over the mountains
Did this sly bold Reynardine.

End of Act Two